CATALOGUE

OF

PORTRAITS

IN

INDEPENDENCE HALL,

PHILADELPHIA.

CATALOGUE

OF THE

NATIONAL PORTRAITS

IN

INDEPENDENCE HALL;

COMPRISING THOSE OF MANY OF

The Signers of the Declaration of Independence,

AND OF OTHER DISTINGUISHED PERSONS.

PHILADELPHIA:
PUBLISHED FOR THE USE OF VISITERS.
1871.

INTRODUCTION.

This rare and valuable collection of NATIONAL PORTRAITS has been procured by the city Councils under many disadvantages. They have been gathered from various localities throughout the Republic, at considerable cost, and are here brought together as at the common centre of the nation. Hither came the men of the original national compact, pledging to each other, before God, their best exertions for the good of mankind, and here we reverently place their shadows for the loving homage of succeeding generations.

The series exhibits almost the only authentic portraits extant of their illustrious originals, in whom, not Americans only, but all the good and true of the world should take an abiding interest.

In addition to the Portraits there are many other objects in the Hall which cannot fail to attract attention; among which may be named as prominent—the old BELL of Independence; a portion of a PEW in Christ Church used by General Washington, General Lafayette, and Benjamin Franklin; the CHAIR in which John Hancock sat as president of Congress, two CHAIRS of members of the same, and the small mahogany TABLE on which the Declaration of Independence was signed; a portion of the stone STEP from which Independence was proclaimed: and Rush's STATUE of Washington. In the centre of the Hall, suspended from the ceiling, is the ancient CHANDELIER which was used by Congress during its deliberations, and more particularly on the night prior to the passage of the Declaration.

There is also a CHAIR, made in 1828 by order of the commissioners of the late District of Kensington, which forms in itself quite a museum of curiosities. Among the materials used in its construction will be found a portion of a mahogany beam from a house built in 1496, near the present city of St. Domingo, for the use of Christopher Columbus, being the first house built in America by European hands. This chair also contains fragments of the Treaty Elm Tree; of Penn's Cottage in Letitia Court; of the United States Frigate Constitution; of the Ship-of-the-line Pennsylvania; and of one of a group of Walnut Trees which formerly stood in front of the State House which was then out of town! Some portions of cane-seating from a chair once the property of William Penn, and a lock of the hair of the late Chief Justice Marshal, are also inserted in this curious piece of furniture.

SIGNERS OF THE DECLARATION OF INDEPENDENCE.

NAME AND BIRTHPLACE.	AGE IN 1776.	DATE OF DEATH	AGE.
John Morton, Delaware,	41	April, 1777,	43
Button Gwinnet, England,	42	May 27, 1777,	44
Philip Livingston, New York,	60	June 12, 1778,	62
John Hart, New Jersey,	66	——1776,	70
Joseph Hewes, New Jersey	—	November 10, 1779,	—
Thomas Lynch, South Carolina,	27	Close of 1779,	30
Richard Stockton, New Jersey,	45	——1781,	50
Cesar Rodney, Delaware,	47	June 26, 1784.	55
Stephen Hopkins, Rhode Island,	69	July 13, 1785,	78
William Whipple, Massachusetts,	45	November 28, 1785,	54
Thomas Stone, Maryland,	32	——1787,	43
Arthur Middleton, S. Carolina,	37	January 1, 1788,	49
John Penn, Virginia,	34	September, 1788,	46
Benjamin Franklin, Mass.,	70	April 17, 1790,	84
Lyman Hall, South Carolina,	46	——1790,	60
William Hooper, Mass,.	34	——1790,	48
Francis Hopkinson, Penna.,	37	May 9, 1791,	52
Roger Sherman, Mass.,	55	July 26, 1793,	72
John Hancock, Mass.,	39	October 8, 1793,	56
Richard Henry Lee, Virginia,	44	June 22, 1794,	62
Abraham Clark, New Jersey,	50	Autumn, 1794	64
John Witherspoon, Scotland,	54	November 15, 1794,	72
Josiah Bartlett, Massachusetts,	46	May 19, 1795.	65
Samuel Huntington, Connecticut,	43	January 5, 1796,	63
Oliver Wolcott, Connecticut,	51	December 1, 1796,	71
Francis L. Lee, Virginia,	40	April, 1797,	63
Carter Braxton, Virginia,	40	October 10, 1798,	61
James Wilson, Scotland,	33	August 28, 1795,	55
George Read, Maryland,	42	Autumn, 1798,	64
William Paca, Maryland,	36	——1799,	—
Edward Rutledge, S. Carolina,	26	January 28, 1800,	50
Matthew Thornton, Ireland,	61	June 24, 1803,	88
Francis Lewis, Wales,	62	December 13, 1803,	81
Samuel Adams, Massachusetts,	54	October 2, 1803,	81
George Walton, Virginia,	36	February 2, 1804,	64
Robert Morris, England,	42	May 8, 1806,	72
George Wythe, Virginia,	50	June 8, 1806,	80
Thomas Heyward, S. Carolina,	30	March, 1808,	63
Samuel Chase, Maryland,	35	June 17, 1811,	—
William Williams, Connecticut,	45	August 2, 1811.	80
George Clymer, Pennsylvania,	36	January 28, 1813,	73
Benjamin Rush, Pennsylvania,	30	April 19, 1813,	67
Robert T. Paine, Massachusetts,	46	May 11, 1814,	84
Elbridge Gerry, Massachusetts.	31	November 23, 1814,	69
Thomas McKean, Pennsylvania,	42	June 24, 1817,	83
William Ellery, Rhode Island,	68	February 15, 1820,	92
William Floyd, New York,	42	August 1, 1821,	87
Thomas Jefferson, Virginia,	33	July 4, 1826,	83
John Adams, Massachusetts,	40	July 4, 1826,	90
Charles Carroll, Maryland,	38	November 1805,	95
Benjamin Harrison, Virginia,	36	April, 1791,	51
Thomas Nelson, Jr., Virginia,	38	January 4, 1789,	51
James Smith, Pennsylvania,	57	July 11, 1806,	87
George Taylor, Pennsylvania,	60	February 23, 1781,	65
George Ross, Pennsylvania,	46	July 1779,	49
Lewis Morris, New York,	50	January 27, 1798,	72

George Clinton, *Henry Wisner* and *Robert H. Livingston*, all of New York, were present on the 4th of July, and voted for Independence; but were not present when the Declaration was engrossed for signature, and thus never signed it, though Mr. Livingston was one of the committee of five that reported the instrument.

THE STATE HOUSE.

(From Watson's Annals.)

This celebrated building was commenced in 1729 and completed in 1734. The amplitude of such an edifice, in so early a day, and the expensive interior decorations, at a cost of five thousand six hundred pounds, are creditable evidences of the liberality and public spirit of the times.

The place is consecrated by numerous facts in our colonial and revolutionary history, whose contemplation fills the mind with numerous associations and local impressions. Within its walls were witnessed many memorable doings of our spirited forefathers; above all, it was made renowned in 1776, as possessing beneath its dome the Hall of Independence, in which the representatives of a nation resolved to be free and independent. Within this sacred Hall, in committee of the whole, the Declaration was passed and signed, and from the yard proclaimed to the world.

THE OLD BELL OF INDEPENDENCE.

This Bell was imported from England in 1752, for the State House; but, having met with some accident in the trial ringing after it was landed, it lost the tone received in the father-land, and had to be conformed to ours by a re-casting. This was done under the direction of Isaac Norris, Esq., then Speaker of the Colonial Assembly; and to him we are probably indebted for the remarkable motto so indicative of its future use.—"PROCLAIM LIBERTY THROUGHOUT ALL THE LAND UNTO ALL THE INHABITANTS THEREOF."—Lev. xxv. 10.

That it was adopted from Scripture, may to many be still more impressive, as being also the voice of God—of that great Arbiter by whose signal providence we afterwards attained to that 'Liberty' and self-government which bids fair to emancipate our whole continent, and in time to influence and meliorate the condition of the subjects of arbitrary government throughout the civilized world.—WATSON'S ANNALS.

CATALOGUE.

1. *William Penn,* the proprietor of Pennsylvania, and founder of the city of Philadelphia, born in England October fourteenth, 1644; died on the thirtieth of July, 1718; was buried without pomp or useless display, at the secluded village of Jordans, Buckinghamshire, on the fifth of August, 1718. He was one of the most celebrated men of the age in which he lived, and his name will be immortal. INMAN.

2. *John Hancock,* born in Massachusetts, 1737. President of the illustrious Congress which declared American Independence; died in October, 1793, in his fifty-sixth year. C. W. PEALE.

3. *Robert Morris,* one of the signers of the Declaration of Independence; the great American financier, of whom it was said—"The Americans owed, and still owe, as much acknowledgment to the financial operations of Robert Morris, as to the negotiations of Benjamin Franklin, or even to the arms of George Washington."

C. W. PEALE.

4. *General Joseph Reed,* of Philadelphia, a distinguished lawyer, patriot, and statesman; Adjutant General on the staff of General Washington: was President of Pennsylvania from 1778 until his death in 1781.

C. W. PEALE.

5. *Thomas Jefferson,* of Virginia, third President of the United States, and author of the Declaration of Independence: born in 1743, (O. S.) died at Monticello, July 4, 1826. C. W. PEALE.

6. *Doctor John Witherspoon,* born in Scotland in 1722. He was a descendant of the Reverend John Knox, the great Scotch Reformer; was a signer of the Declaration of Independence, and President of Princeton College, New Jersey. C. W. PEALE.

7. *Philip Livingston,* one of the signers of the Declaration of Independence; a man who filled many distinguished positions prior to the Revolution; was a humble Christian and an honest man: born at Albany, New York, on the fifteenth of January, 1716; died on the 12th of June, 1778, at York, Pennsylvania. C.W. PEALE.

8. *Richard Henry Lee,* of Virginia; an eloquent and able politician, one of the signers of the Declaration of Independence, a member of the first Congress at Philadelphia, President of Congress, member of the Convention which framed the Constitution of the United States; Senator in Congress; an able writer and brilliant speaker: born in Virginia, 1722, died on the nineteenth of June, 1794. C W. PEALE.

9. *Samuel Huntington,* of Connecticut, a signer of the Declaration of Independence; succeeded John Jay as President of Congress; was also Governor of Connecticut. C.W. PEALE.

10. *Charles Carroll,* of Carrollton, the latest survivor of the signers of the Declaration of Independence, full of years and full of honors, closed his earthly career on the fourteenth of November, 1832. A nation's tears were shed upon his grave—a nation's gratitude hallows his memory. C.W. PEALE.

11. *Francis Hopkinson,* one of the signers of the Declaration of Independence; born in Philadelphia in 1738; a lawyer of distinction and for many years Judge of the Admiralty Court of the United States for Pennsylvania; (he was the father of the late Judge Joseph Hop-

kinson, a very eminent lawyer, politician and writer;) died suddenly May 9, 1791. DUBOIS.

12. *Samuel Chase,* an Associate Justice of the Supreme Court of the United States; also a signer of the Declaration of Independence; born in Maryland, 1741, and died on the nineteenth of June, 1811. C. W. PEALE.

13. *Thomas McKean,* of Pennsylvania; a signer of the Declaration of Independence; an eminent jurist; Chief Justice of the Supreme Court of Pennsylvania, also Governor of that State. C. W. PEALE.

14. *The Marquis de Lafayette,* born at the chateau de Chavagnac, in the province of Auvergne, France, September 6th, 1757; died at his hotel in Paris, May 21st, 1834. An apostle of true liberty and a companion of Washington in the Revolution. T. SULLY.

15. *Dr. Benjamin Rush,* the celebrated physician, writer, and teacher of medicine; was a member of Congress from Pennsylvania in 1776; one of the signers of the Declaration of Independence; born near Philadelphia, on the twenty-fourth of December, 1745; died April nineteenth, 1813. C. W. PEALE.

16. *John Adams,* a member of Congress from Massachusetts in 1776: a signer of the Declaration of Independence, and second president of the United States; born at Quincy, near Boston, on the nineteenth of October, 1735, (o.s.) died on the fourth of July, 1826.

C. W. PEALE.

17. *Hernando Cortez,* a distinguished Spanish commander, conqueror of Mexico; born in the province of Estremadura; studied law at the University of Salamanca, entered the army, and was sent to St. Domingo in 1504; died in Spain in 1554, aged sixty-nine years.

C. W. PEALE.

18. *Constantine Francis Chassbouf,* Count de Volney, an eminent French writer and traveller.

C. W. PEALE.

19. *Robert Fulton,* the successful inventor of steamboat navigation; born in Lancaster county, Pennsylvania, about 1760: died suddenly February 24, 1815.

C. W. PEALE.

20. *General Count Rochambault,* commander-in-chief of the French army engaged in the American Revolution. C. W. PEALE.

21. *Colonel James Wilkinson,* of the army of the Revolution; afterwards Major General in the United States army. C. W. PEALE.

22. *Robert Wharton,* an eminent citizen of Philadelphia, and for many years distinguished for his firmness and efficiency as mayor of that city. C. W. PEALE.

23. *Admiral Penn,* father of the illustrious William Penn, proprietor of Pennsylvania and founder of the city of Philadelphia. C. W. PEALE.

24. *General Du Portail,* a distinguished officer in the French army in the American Revolution. C.W. PEALE.

25. *Captain Nicholas Biddle,* a distinguished naval commander during the war of the Revolution, who performed many brilliant exploits, and was killed in action in 1778. C. W. PEALE.

26. *Colonel De Cambray,* of the French army during the war of the Revolution. C. W. PEALE.

27. *General Benjamin Lincoln,* of the army of the Revolution; born at Hingham, Massachusetts, January 23d, 1733, (o.s.) died on the 9th of May, 1810.

C. W. PEALE.

28. *John Page,* of Virginia; a patriot, statesman, and Christian; one of the first representatives in Congress under the Constitution; also Governor of Virginia.

C. W. PEALE.

29. *Captain Meriweather Lewis,* a native of Virginia, and Captain in the United States army, associated with Captain Clark in the exploring expedition to the mouth of the Columbia river; afterwards appointed Governor of the Territory of Louisiana. C. W. PEALE.

30. *Christopher Gadsden,* born in South Carolina in 1734; was the originator of the "Liberty Tree" in America. When Major Andre was executed, General Gadsden was tauntingly admonished to prepare for death, as he would be made the retaliatory sacrifice. He firmly replied, "I am always prepared to die for my country." He died in 1805. C. W. PEALE.

31. *Colonel Samuel Smith,* of Maryland, distinguished himself during the war of the Revolution by a gallant defence of Mud Island, afterwards called Fort Mifflin, near Philadelphia; for many years a leading politician, and Senator in Congress. C. W. PEALE.

32. *Colonel John Eager Howard,* of Maryland, and of the army of the Revolution; distinguished for valor and activity during the whole of the war, but particularly at the battle of the Cowpens; afterwards Governor of Maryland and Senator in Congress. C. W. PEALE.

33. *Colonel Henry Lee,* one of the most celebrated officers of the American Revolution, commander of the legion known by his name; a daring and active partizan; author of Memoirs of the War of the Revolution, in the southern department; member of Congress; Governor of Virginia: pronounced an eulogy on Washington before Congress, in which he used the words, since so celebrated: "First in war, first in peace, and first in the hearts of his countrymen." C. W. PEALE.

34. *Chevalier de la Luzerne,* second Minister from France to the United States. C. W. PEALE.

35. *John Dickinson,* a distinguished patriot and writer; member of Congress in 1774; President of Pennsylvania in 1782; afterwards President of Delaware; author of "Letters of a Pennsylvania Farmer."

C. W. PEALE.

36. *Brandt.* (Indian Chief.)

37. *Alexander Hamilton,* chief author of the Constitution of the United States, and first Secretary of the national treasury. Born January 11, 1757, in the Island of Nevis, British West Indies. Killed July 12, 1804. C. W. PEALE.

38. *Charles Thomson,* Secretary of Congress during the Revolution; a man of ardent patriotism, excellent personal character, and pure morals; his love of truth was so inviolable as to become proverbial: "As true as if Charles Thomson had said it." C. W. PEALE.

39. *Timothy Pickering,* of Massachusetts, Colonel and Adjutant General in the Revolutionary army; was successively Postmaster General, Secretary of War, and Secretary of State; Senator in Congress: distinguished for firmness, energy, activity and disinterestedness.

C. W. PEALE

40. *Commodore Hazlewood,* an active naval officer in the Revolution. C. W. PEALE.

41. *John Andrew Shulze,* Governor of Pennsylvania; a man of liberal education and excellent moral character. R. PEALE.

42. *Red Jacket.* The celebrated Indian Chief Red Jacket was born about the year 1756, at "Old Castle," now embraced in the town of Seneca, Ontario county, New York, three miles west of the village of Geneva. His Indian name was LA-GO-YOU-WAT-HA, or "Keeper Awake;" he got the name of Red Jacket from wearing a

scarlet coat, richly embroidered, presented to him by British officers during the war of the Revolution. He was a war chief of the Senecas, and died at his residence, near Buffalo, New York, on the 20th of January, 1836. Washington presented Red Jacket with a medal in 1792, which he ever afterwards wore, having never been seen without it. He fought under the British standard in the American Revolution. C. W. PEALE.

43. *Doctor Benjamin Franklin*, the great philosopher and statesman, born in Boston, Massachusetts, January 17, 1706; died April 17, 1790, and lies buried in Christ Church burying ground, at the corner of Arch street and fifth, Philadelphia. C. W. PEALE.

44. *Colonel Stephen H. Long,* of the United States Topographical Engineers; commanded in two exploring expeditions to the sources of the Mississippi, and to the Rocky Mountains. C. W. PEALE.

45. *Peyton Randolph,* of Virginia, an eminent lawyer and statesman, President of the first American Congress. C. W. PEALE.

46. *William Moore,* President of the State of Pennsylvania in 1781; an excellent man.

C. W. PEALE.

47. *General Nathaniel Green,* commander-in-chief of the Southern Department in the Revolution.

C. W. PEALE.

48. *General James M. Varnum,* a Major General in the Revolution; a member of Congress from Rhode Island; died at Marietta, Ohio, 1789.

C. W. PEALE.

49. *Doctor Robert Hare,* of Philadelphia, an eminent chemist; Professor of Chemistry in the Medical Department of the University of Pennsylvania.

R. PEALE.

50. *General Charles Lee,* of the Revolution; was a native of North Wales, and held a military commission at the age of eleven; served while young in Canada; and under Burgoyne in Portugal; in the Polish army; travelled the tour of Europe; killed an Italian officer in a duel; came to America in 1773; declared for liberty, and was made a Major General by Congress in 1775. He commanded for a time in New York; then in the South, and was afterwards transferred to New Jersey: he died in October, 1782, in Philadelphia.

C. W. PEALE.

51. *Henry Laurens,* of South Carolina, member of Congress in 1776 and President of that body. In 1779 was sent as Minister to Holland, and on his way thither captured by the British, committed to the Tower Prison and confined fourteen months. In 1782, he signed the Treaty of Peace with Great Britain. C. W. PEALE.

52. *Robert Morris,* the Financier of the Revolution.

C. W. PEALE.

53. *Albert Gallatin,* a celebrated banker. Born in Switzerland but mainly resident in New York.

C. W. PEALE.

54. *Captain James Biddle,* of Philadelphia, born on the eighteenth of February, 1783; was a distinguished officer of the war of 1812. C. W. PEALE.

55. *Commodore Stephen Decatur* was born on the fifth of January, 1779, on the eastern shore of Maryland: he entered the navy in 1798, and soon arrived at distinction; commanded the frigate United States, and captured the British frigate Macedonian.

J. STUART.

56. *Colonel Nathaniel Ramsay,* a native of Maryland, an officer of the Revolutionary army, afterwards

Collector of the port of Baltimore; a true patriot and a good man. C. W. PEALE.

57. *William Bartram,* of Philadelphia, a distinguished naturalist and botanist; author of a work on Ornithology, and of travels in Florida. C. W. PEALE.

58. *Baron Frederick William Steuben,* a Major General in the American army during the Revolution; was a Prussian officer who served many years in the armies of Frederick the Great; was one of his aids, and held the rank of Lieutenant General. He arrived in New Hampshire from Marseilles, in November, 1777, with strong recommendations to Congress; claimed no rank, and only requested permission to render, as a volunteer, what services he could to the American army. He was soon appointed to the office of Inspector General with the rank of Major General, and established a uniform system of manœuvres during the continuance of the troops at Valley Forge, and effected a most important change in all ranks of the army. He volunteered in the action at Monmouth, and commanded in the trenches of Yorktown, on the day which concluded the struggle with Great Britain. He died at Steubenville, N. Y., November 28, 1794, aged sixty-one years. An accomplished gentleman and virtuous citizen, of extensive knowledge and sound judgment. C. W. PEALE.

59. *General Arthur St. Clair,* of the army of the Revolution; commander-in-chief of the North Western Army and Governor of the North Western Territory.

C. W. PEALE.

60. *Chevalier Gerard,* first Minister from France to the United States; a man of high attainments, and exceedingly popular during his residence in this country.

C. W. PEALE.

61. *Colonel William A. Washington,* a chivalrous officer of the Revolution. He defeated the celebrated Tarleton in South Carolina; and was a relative of him who was "first in the hearts of his countrymen."

C. W. PEALE.

62. *General Artemas Ward,* of Massachusetts, Major General in the army of the Revolution, member of Congress before and after the adoption of the Constitution; died at Shrewsbury, October 28, 1800, aged seventy-three years. C. W. PEALE.

63. *Timothy Matlack,* a public-spirited and highly esteemed citizen of Philadelphia, who, without being in office, was active in public affairs, during and after the Revolution. He lived to an advanced age, and possessed a remarkable recollection of past events.

C. W. PEALE.

64. *Charles Thomson,* Secretary of the Congress which declared American Independence. C. W. PEALE.

65. *Francis John,* Marquis de Chastellux, a French Field Marshal, author of "Travels in North America;" an able writer. C. W. PEALE.

66. *Colonel David Humphreys,* of Connecticut, a distinguished patriot, soldier, and author; aid-de-camp to general Washington; Secretary of Legation at Paris; Ambassador to the court of Lisbon; Minister to Spain.

R. PEALE.

67. *General Lachlan McIntosh,* of the Revolution, member of Congress from Georgia in 1784. C. W. PEALE.

68. *Reverend Bishop White,* Chaplain to the Congress which declared American Independence, and senior Bishop of the Protestant Episcopal Church in the United States. C. W. PEALE.

69. *Mrs. Robert Morris,* wife of the great financier, daughter of Colonel White and sister of Bishop White. She was married in 1769. Her name was Mary.

C. W. PEALE.

70. *David Rittenhouse,* a celebrated American mathematician: born in Pennsylvania in 1732. After the Revolution he was Director of the Mint, Treasurer of Pennsylvania, and President of the American Philosophical Society. C. W. PEALE

71. *Lady Martha Washington,* wife of General George Washington; was born in New Kent, Colony of Virginia, in May, 1732; died at Mount Vernon, in the seventy-first year of her age. C. W. PEALE.

72. *General George Washington,* (in Jacquard,) This portrait was woven at Lyons, France, in silk, in the Jacquard loom of Messrs. Pons, Philippe & Vibert; and by them presented to the city of Philadelphia.

73. *Rev. Dr. Henry Muhlenberg,* of Lancaster, Pennsylvania, a learned naturalist, and correspondent of most of the distinguished botanists of Europe. C.W. PEALE.

74. *Commodore David Porter,* of the United States Navy, born in Boston on February first, 1780. He was a brave and gallant officer. He resigned his commission in the navy and was appointed charge-d'-affaires at Constantinople; he subsequently returned to America, and was sent out as full minister to the Porte, and died March 28, 1843. His remains were brought to Philadelphia and interred there. C. W. PEALE.

75. *General William Smallwood,* of the Revolution; Governor of Maryland; was a trne patriot and worthy citizen. C. W. PEALE.

76. *Baron De Kalb,* of the army of the Revolution, born in Germany; served in the French army forty-two years; commanded the right wing of the American army

and was killed at Camden, S. C., 1778. The success of the American arms owed much to the system of discipline introduced by this officer. C. W. PEALE.

77. *General John Armstrong,* an officer of the Revolution; Minister to France; Secretary of War under James Madison in 1813. R. PEALE.

78. *Doctor William Shippen,* an eminent physician of Philadelphia, one of the founders of and early professors in the Medical Department of the University of Pennsylvania. R. PEALE.

79. *General Andrew Jackson,* seventh President of the United States and hero of New Orleans; born on the fifteenth of March, 1767, in Waxaw, South Carolina, and died June 8, 1845. ETTER.

80. *Brigadier Gen. Zebulon Montgomery Pike,* born at Lamberton, New Jersey; fell at the capture of York, Upper Canada, April 27, 1813. He was considered one of the best disciplinarians of the army of the United States. His death was a great public misfortune.

C. W. PEALE.

81. *Jonathan Bayard Smith,* of Philadelphia, a distinguished classical scholar, member of Congress in the Revolution, Colonel in the army at Princeton, Trenton, and Brandywine. He was a true patriot, ardently attached to his country, and a man of pure moral character. C. W. PEALE.

82. *Governor William Finley,* United States Senator and Governor of Pennsylvania. He was a modest, unassuming gentleman and a most excellent officer.

C. W. PEALE.

83. *Colonel Tennent,* a French officer who served in the army of the Revolution; returned to France, and came as Minister of France to the United States.

C. W. PEALE.

84. *General Daniel Morgan,* of the army of the Revolution. He organized a celebrated rifle corps, and was of great service during the war. C. W. PEALE.

85. *Governor Simon Snyder,* Governor of the State of Pennsylvauia for three terms. A man much esteemed for his honesty and good intentions, and a most worthy citizen. C. W. PEALE.

86. *William Findlay,* of Westmoreland County, Pennsylvania; one of the framers of the constitution of that State; and member of Congress from the above county. Also author of a history of the western rebellion, or "Whisky Insurrection;" lived to an advanced age, and died much lamented by numerous friends. C.W.PEALE.

87. *General Henry Dearborn,* of New Hampshire, a gallant officer in the Revolution, Secretary of War, Major General in the United States army in the war of 1812. C. W. PEALE.

88. *Elias Boudinot,* an eminent writer and philanthropist; Commissary General of Prisoners during the Revolution. In 1777, a member of Congress, and in 1782, president of that body. Succeeded Rittenhouse as Director of the Mint; was the first president of the American Bible Society, and a munificent patron of that and other charities. C. W. PEALE.

89. *Doctor John Hanson,* President of the Old Confederacy: a statesman and patriot. C. W. PEALE.

90. *Rufus King,* an eminent statesman and diplomatist; born in Maine, 1755; member of Congress in 1784; Minister to England; for many years Senator in Congress from New York. A man of superior abilities, and exhibiting an ardent attachment to the institutions of his country. C. W. PEALE.

91. *General Henry Knox,* of the army of the Revolution and Secretary of War in 1789; a brave and gal-

lant officer, who was much beloved by the commander-in-chief, General George Washington. C. W. PEALE.

92. *Colonel T. Forrest,* of the army of the Revolution; distinguished for his bravery, and was much esteemed by General Lafayette. C. W. PEALE.

93. *General Otho Williams,* of Maryland, a distinguished officer in the army of the Revolution; in which he obtained the rank of Brigadier General. He was indefatigable and persevering, and rendered important services to his country. C. W. PEALE.

94. *General Sumter,* of the Revolutionary army; a native of South Carolina. He was a true patriot, and enthusiastic in the cause of liberty. C. W. PEALE.

95. *General William Clark,* who was associated with Captain Lewis in the exploring expedition to the mouth of the Columbia river: afterwards Governor of the Territory of Missouri, and superintendent of Indian Affairs, and Surveyor General of Public Lands at St. Louis. C. W. PEALE.

96. *General Horatio Gates,* the hero of Saratoga; a brave and useful officer. C. W. PEALE.

97. *Dr. David Ramsey,* author of a history of the American Revolution, member of Congress from South Carolina in 1782, 1783, 1785 and 1786. He was an able and useful member of that body, and ardently attached to his country. C. W. PEALE.

98. *Count Real,* an officer of distinction, during the Revolutionary War. C. W. PEALE.

99. *Captain Joshua Barney,* a distinguished naval commander in the Revolution, and also in the war of 1812. He was forty-one years in the service of the U.S. and in twenty-six battles. At his death he was Collector of the port of Baltimore. C. W. PEALE.

100. *Commodore John Rodgers,* of the United States navy; born in Maryland, 1765; was conspicuous

for brilliant exploits during a long career; was a brave and humane officer. C. W. PEALE.

101. *Governor Joseph Hiester,* Governor of Pennsylvania; was a modest, unassuming man, much esteemed by his fellow citizens. C. W. PEALE.

102. *Captain John Paul Jones,* the celebrated naval hero, who performed many gallant actions in the service of the American people, in the War of the Revolution. Born at Arbigland, Scotland, July, 1747. Died at Paris, 1792. He was one of the most courageous and determined commanders that ever lived. C. W. PEALE.

103. *General Richard Montgomery,* born 1737; fell in the attack of Quebec, L. C., December 31, 1775. C. W. PEALE.

104. *General Joseph Warren.* This was the first officer of distinction immolated on the altar of freedom, at the dawn of the Revolution which ended in the recognition of the independence of the thirteen United States of America by Great Britain. Of his character it may be said, that to the purest patriotism and most undaunted bravery, he added the best virtues of domestic life, the eloquence of an accomplished orator, and the wisdom of an able statesman. His fame will be immortal. C. W. PEALE.

105. *General Thomas Mifflin,* a Major General in the army of the Revolution, a member of the Convention which framed the Constitution of the United States; President of the Executive Council of Philadelphia, and Governor of Pennsylvania after the adoption of the Constitution. He was an eloquent speaker and able statesman. C. W. PEALE.

106. *William Rush,* was born in Philadelphia on July fourth, 1756. He entered Washington's army in the earliest part of the conflict for Independence, and

was honored with high favor from the commander-in-chief during and after the war. His profession, on giving up the military, was that of a sculptor in wood; and he attained to high excellence in the same, executing many beautiful works, principal among which is the full length statue of Washington in Independence Hall. The city honored him with a position in her Councils as a member, which he filled with distinction for more than a quarter of a century. Mr. Rush died January twenty-seventh, 1833. C. W. PEALE.

107. This PROMETHOTYPE represents that distinguished citizen and statesman, Henry Clay. HAYNE.

108. *General George Washington.* This portrait was copied by Woodside from Stuart's. The frame was made in the public streets of Philadelphia, by the journeymen cabinet makers of that city, in the procession commemorative of the centennial anniversary of Washington's birth.

109. *General George Washington.* This portrait was taken by Mr. James Peale in Philadelphia. The frame was made by order of the late Alderman Binns, from timber taken from the hull of the old frigate Constitution. J. PEALE.

110. A colored drawing representing a Triumphal Arch which was erected at the corner of Fourth and Tammany streets, on the occasion of General Lafayette's visit to Philadelphia, in September, 1824.

111. This engraving of Washington's Farewell Address, printed on satin, was presented by Mr. B. H. Rand, of Philadelphia.

112. *Roger Sherman,* one of the signers of the Declaration of Independence. His father was a farmer at Newtown, Mass., where Roger Sherman was born on the 19th of April, 1721. He was twice married, and was the father of fifteen children. He was a member of

Congress from 1774 till 1782; and in 1791 he was elected to the Senate of the United States. He died on the 23d of July, 1793, in his seventy-third year.

113. *General George Washington.* A photographic likeness, by W. Germon, Esq., from Stuart's painting now in the Athenæum at Boston; presented to the city of Philadelphia, July 4th, 1856.

114. An engraving of Penn's Treaty with the Indians, on the banks of the Delaware, 1682.

115. *William White, D.D.* late Bishop of the Protestant Episcopal Church of the State of Pennsylvania, and Chaplain to the Congress of the United States.

116. *William Alexander, Lord Sterling,* Major General in the Revolutionary army; distinguished himself in the battles of Brandywine and Germantown; also at Monmouth. He was a gallant and meritorious officer, and rendered great service to the cause of liberty. He died much regretted at Albany, January, 1783. OTIS.

117. *Richard Dobbs Spaight,* (likeness in crayon) Governor of North Carolina; one of the patriots of the Revolution; a member of the convention which framed the Constitution of the United States, and a personal friend of Washington.

118. *George Reade,* a signer of the Declaration of Independence, U. S. Senator, and Chief Justice of Delaware. Born in Maryland, 1734; died in 1798.

119. *Elbridge Gerry,* a signer of the Declaration of Independence and Vice President of U.S. in 1812. Born at Marblehead, Massachusetts, July, 1744; died in 1812.

120. *William Bradford,* an eminent lawyer of Pennsylvania, and Attorney General of United States. Born September, 1755; died August, 1795.

121. *General W. H. Harrison,* a distinguished officer in the War of 1812, and President of the United States in 1841.

122. *Lieut. J. T. Greble,* U.S.A. One of the earliest victims of the great Rebellion. He fell at Great Bethel, June 10, 1861. E. D. MARCHANT.

123. *General George G. Meade,* Major General in the army of the U. S. and Commander-in-chief of the army of the Potomac at the battle of Gettysburg, and until its disbandment at the close of the war. LAMBDIN.

124. *General U. S. Grant,* Generalissimo of the National army by special act of Congress, and President of the United States since March 4, 1869. LAMBDIN.

125. *Arthur Lee,* a distinguished Revolutionary patriot and statesman—the youngest of five brothers, all of whom became eminent. He was born in Westmoreland county, Virginia, December 20, 1740, and died December 12, 1792, at his farm on the Rappahannock river, Virginia. C. W. PEALE.

126. *Abraham Lincoln,* sixteenth President of the United States. Elected in November, 1860; re-elected November, 1864; assassinated April 14, 1865.

E. D. MARCHANT.

Thomas Hayward, Jr. of South Carolina, a signer of the Declaration of Independence.

Washington, Lincoln, Grant—"Triumviri Americani." A triple profile medallion in bronze.

MILLER.

Equestrian Portrait of Washington, lately purchased by Councils for the Hall, placed immediately over the entrance. R. PEALE.

A Block of Pennsylvania marble on which is sculptured the coat of arms of the State of Pennsylvania, executed by Mr. W. Struthers for the city of Philadelphia, and intended to form part of the National Washington Monument at Washington City.

Lithograph of the Union Volunteer Refreshment Saloon, foot of Washington street, Philadelphia.

www.ingramcontent.com/pod-product-compliance
Lightning Source LLC
LaVergne TN
LVHW011140110826
845150LV00008B/2440

* 9 7 8 1 4 1 8 1 9 2 6 6 2 *